I care about You

by
Marianne Richmond

I care about You

Marianne Richmond Studios, Inc.
420 N. 5th Street, Suite 840
Minneapolis, MN 55401
www.mariannerichmond.com

ISBN 0-9753528-1-4

Illustrations by Marianne Richmond

Book design by Meg Anderson

Printed in China

First Printing

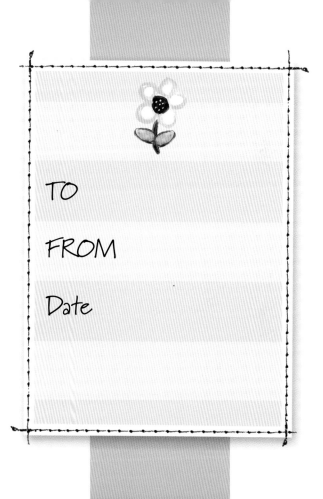

TO

FROM

Date

I know you're going through
a tough time right now,
and I want you to know I care.

I can't say I know
exactly how you feel.

What I can say is,
"I am here for you."

To hold your hand.

To listen without judging.

To offer an opinion if you want one.

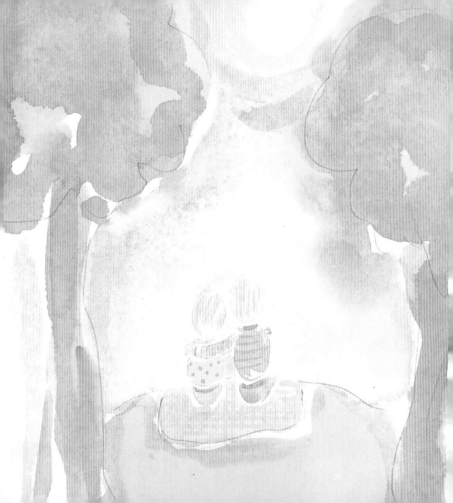

To hug you if you want to cry.

I want to give you a break —
to take you to the movies...
or out for coffee...

so you can think about
something else for a while.

I am here, too,
to simply sit
and quietly
be with you.

I'm committed
to be with you
on your journey.

It's hard to know
why life decides
to challenge us
in the ways
that it does.

We may not
immediately see
the reason
behind our trial.

Or think we
"deserve" our hurt.

That's why I wish you

strength

and wisdom

and perseverance.

I wish you patience
with yourself and
with others who
may not know
what to say.
Or who say the
wrong thing.

Thursday	Friday	Saturday 1
		8
	7	15
6		14
5	13	21

And most of all, I wish you hope.

Hope for a better tomorrow
than your today.

This journey
is your own.
For better
or for worse,
this path is
yours to follow.

But you know what?
It may lead to something
far greater than you
could have imagined.

You may emerge stronger
and braver and more capable
than you ever thought possible.

Sometimes, though, you just
need to know someone is
on your side...

encouraging you,
supporting you,
praying for you.

That someone

is me.

I ask that you help me, too,
by telling me what you need
if I don't seem to be
quite getting it.

Don't burden yourself by thinking
you're asking too much of me.

That's the last thing you need to
concern yourself with.

I really care about you,
and I'm going to
see you through.

A gifted author and artist, Marianne Richmond shares
her creations with millions of people worldwide
through her delightful books, cards, and giftware.
In addition to the *simply said...* and *smartly said...*
gift book series, she has written and illustrated four
additional books: **The Gift of an Angel,
The Gift of a Memory, Hooray for You!** and
The Gifts of Being Grand.

To learn more about Marianne's products, please visit
www.mariannerichmond.com.